THE ART OF
AARDMAN

First published in the United States in 2017 by Chronicle Books LLC.

First published in Great Britain by Simon & Schuster UK Ltd, 2016
A CBS Company.

Library of Congress Cataloging-in-Publication Data available.
ISBN 978-1-4521-6651-3

Printed in China

Designed by Nick Avery Design
Edited by Mandy Archer

10 9 8 7 6 5 4 3 2 1

Chronicle Books LLC
680 Second Street
San Francisco, California 94107
www.chroniclebooks.com

THE ART OF
AARDMAN

THE MAKERS OF *WALLACE & GROMIT,* *CHICKEN RUN,* AND MORE

Foreword by
David Sproxton and Peter Lord

CHRONICLE BOOKS
SAN FRANCISCO

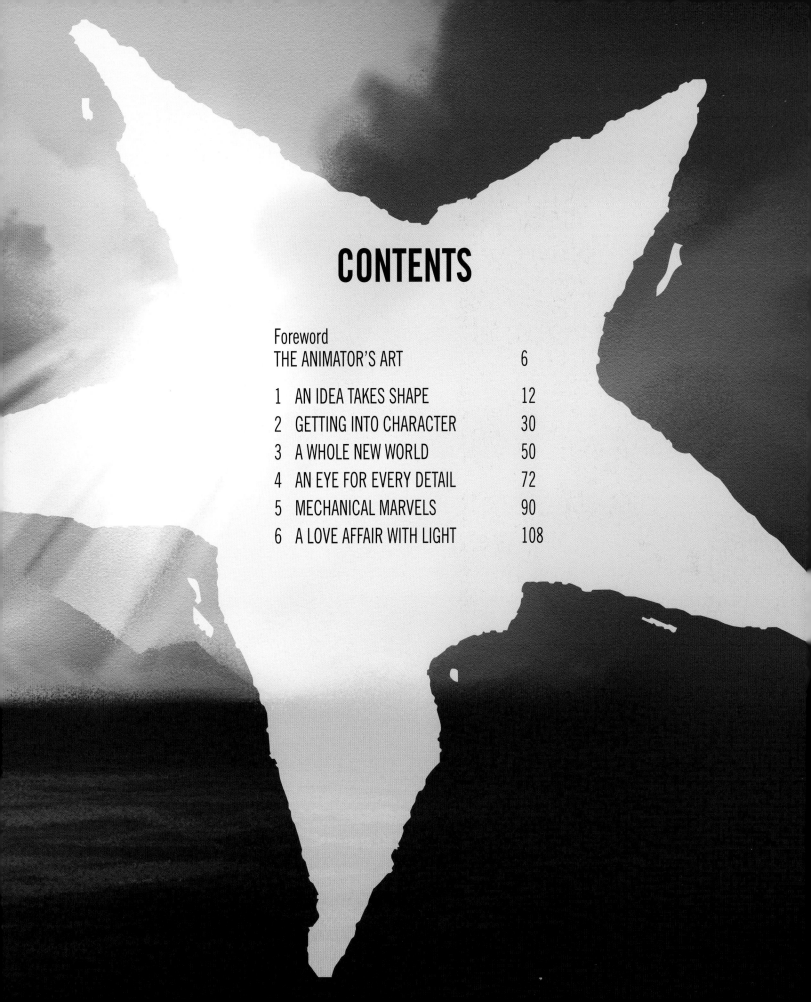

CONTENTS

FOREWORD

THE ANIMATOR'S ART

Facing page:
Peter Lord
Portrait of Nick Park
Sketchbook page

Previous page:
Dominique Louis
Concept art
*The Pirates! In an Adventure
with Scientists!, 2012*

The journey from that first, spontaneous 'what if…?' inkling of an idea to a living, breathing animated film is meandering, precarious and often difficult. Many people join along the way, using their skill and craftmanship to help nurture the idea, develop it and bring it on. Aardman's first such journey began almost 50 years ago, when founders Peter Lord and David Sproxton were schoolboy friends. The film they made was shot in David's family kitchen using a camera borrowed from his dad. A modest beginning, but it was the start of something special. This book is a celebration of all the artists and sculptors whose creativity has made Aardman one of the most loved and respected animation studios in the world.

INTRODUCTION BY
PETER LORD

Welcome to this celebration of Aardman and the amazing artists who have led the creative charge here over the past 40 years.

Almost every film that we bring to the screen has been developed through words and in pictures. And though I'm a big fan of the written word, there's no denying that pictures make for a much more beautiful book. So here we've tried to capture for you the magic, the fun and of course the beauty of the visual side of the process.

We'll take you right through the filmmaking and development process – everything from the first sketch to the finished frame. It all begins in that mysterious time when nothing has been settled, and all possibilities are open. As an artist or an ideas person this is probably the most exciting time you'll have on a new film and I hope that we've managed to communicate some of that energy and sense of adventure. Though some of the pictures you'll see were created a long time ago, this is definitely not an exercise in nostalgia. The same creative process continues here every day as new projects and stories are born. And the work that's being done, by artists old and new, is just as exciting, and just as varied as it's ever been. Many of the people whose work you'll see in this fabulous book are still working away today in sketchbooks or on tablets (or, as in my case, on the back of the agenda for a meeting that isn't really holding my attention). Meanwhile new artists are constantly adding to the story, working out their own personal vision.

I love to dig out the stories within stories and hidden histories buried under the surface. Before any of our finished films are brought to the screen, plenty of words have been written, believe me – countless pages of scripts, notes and analysis. But equally there are hundreds, if not thousands, of images – everything from the faintest pencil sketch to a beautiful digital painting. Through those images, stories are born, characters evolve, jokes are planned and whole worlds are created from scratch. If there's an answer to the old, old question, "where do your ideas come from?" then for me – and for many of us at Aardman – the answer is to be found right here in this book. Ideas come from inside your head, and as often as not, they tumble straight out as drawings and into sketchbooks.

I love to look at early sketches of characters who have now become really well known – like Morph, Rocky the Rooster or Wallace and Gromit. You can see the artists almost dancing around the subject, trying the same thing over and over with tiny variations, then shooting off onto tangents, trying something utterly different – always reaching unconsciously for that magical moment when the image is somehow, magically *right*. I find it fascinating to catch a glimpse of the possibilities that might have been, the characters that never were, the strange ancestors or distant relatives of the familiar screen faces.

When Dave and I first created Morph, we had no clear idea of who he was. Over the years, his character seemed to emerge alongside his appearance, all tied up with the things that he did and the way that he reacted to the world about him. And so much of that took place on paper, through drawing. In two dimensions, we could experiment with Morph's character at the same time as he was finding his feet in three dimensions through animation.

You'll see in these pages many different pictures from 'behind the scenes' – lively sketches, beautiful finished paintings, technical drawings – images that were never designed to appear on screen. But this book is about so much more. It's about the use of colour and light – both crucial parts of storytelling. It's about inventions and inventiveness. It's about character and comedy, mischief and madness. You'll see some glorious, informal photos from the studio floor and other images taken directly from the movies. And these photographs themselves represent an astonishing amount of creative work by scores of people. There are model-makers, carpenters, art directors, puppet-makers, engineers, prop-makers, painters, sculptors – the list goes on and on – not to mention their counterparts who perform almost the same roles but in the world of computer imagery. And then there are those in the camera and lighting department whose job it is to make the sets and characters look as wonderful as they possibly can, and to put them up on screen. An incredible accumulation of talent to transition a world from the drawing board to full three-dimensional reality.

This is a celebration of so many artists, technicians and craftspeople – each with a personal vision, all combining their talents across a huge range of projects, and all linked by the irresistible desire to make the very best, best-looking, funniest films possible.

So, welcome to our world. I hope you enjoy visiting it through these pages as much as I've enjoyed being a part of it. I think you'll find it beautiful and I hope you'll find it inspiring.

"I LOVE TO DIG OUT THE STORIES WITHIN STORIES AND HIDDEN HISTORIES BURIED UNDER THE SURFACE."

INTRODUCTION BY
DAVID SPROXTON

This book is packed full of images, mostly drawn by hand, taken from sketchbooks and our production image banks. But these images are not seen in the final version of the films we make. These images are sketches of ideas, characters and designs which have to be made into real models, sets and props and it is these which are then photographed and become the final film. So the two-dimensional images become three-dimensional objects which are given life by the magic of stop-frame animation. Atmosphere and mood is created very much by the way these objects are photographed, using light and shade.

Most of us take light and lighting for granted, but I found myself intrigued by the properties of light very early on in my life. In fact I can say my love affair with light started at a very tender age, probably when I was about six or seven years old. It happened on one of my trips to the London Science Museum with my parents. I found myself mesmerised by a very simple installation which enabled me to change the mood of a small model depicting a scene from Shakespeare's play, *Julius Caesar*. Nothing changed except the colour and direction of the lighting, yet the emotional impact of the scene changed totally. I found the whole thing fascinating, although I didn't quite know why at the time.

I became intrigued with lighting, making small lights from old drink cans and playing with things like back projection. I recall taking photographs, on a plate camera, of my toy soldiers set up in small battle scene, and trying to make it look as realistic as possible. I found myself fascinated by the way in which static, miniature models could be made to look realistic and full of action in a photograph. I think I enjoyed both the mood that could be created through lighting and the sense of illusion. I liked the idea that what you see is a construct, not reality at all. It is all just props, painted wood and lighting put together to create a scene with a certain mood and character. Film and theatre sets are constructed illusions like this and stop-frame films are made in the same way with the added illusion of creating movement where there is none in reality.

Whilst at college I spent considerable time lighting student stage shows, introducing me to many tools and techniques which have stood me in good stead ever since. Importantly, it also taught me about working with a team, taking a director's brief and meeting a deadline!

The legacy of this experience is that a theatre lighting designer would find him or herself very much at home in the Aardman studios, as we have adopted much of the technology used in the theatre, giving us very finely tuned control of our lamps and lighting.

I would be the first to admit that the lighting and photography of our early work was somewhat rudimentary and functional. This was partly the result of having to match our footage with video material shot in a television studio, which tended to use rather flat lighting. It was also because I was still very much learning my craft and we had rather rudimentary equipment. But when I could I would try to make the lighting more cinematic or at least have a definite sense of light and shade. I always felt that we were film-makers first and foremost, and although we made our films in a rather archane and laborious way, there was no reason at all why we shouldn't attempt to make them look as dramatic and moody as full blown live- action films.

That initial experience at the Science Museum illustrated very effectively the power of lighting, in the form of light, shade and colour, to trigger an innate or learned emotional response in an audience, and that is very much what the job of a Director of Photography or Lighting Cameraman is all about. Horror films are usually set at night because we still harbour fears of the dark deep in our minds. Sunny scenes generally engender a sense of wellbeing and energy. The use of unnatural colours in lighting can make us feel uncomfortable. One of the key questions a DoP will ask is, "what time of day is the scene set in?" We all know intuitively what morning light is like, how the sun sets and what moonlight is. We can recreate these effects on a set and thus trigger an understanding of the time of day and mood very easily in the audience.

Each production presents its own set of challenges for the DoP, for example, how to achieve the effect of rain running down a window or how to balance the lighting with characters having bright white bodies but pitch black faces, in the case of Shaun the Sheep. There is always extensive photographic testing carried out before a production starts, to check that colours can be rendered accurately, that costumes stand out against backgrounds, and a lighting style established that can be used throughout the film.

Generally, our DoPs apply the same thinking to their craft as their live-action counterparts. "Lighting for the shadows" is a phrase often heard amongst DoPs. What this means is that lights are placed not so much to illuminate, but to produce shadows which give shape and form to the models. In our world of puppets and models, giving volume and dimension to our characters is important and that is achieved by placing lights to give shape and shade.

Over the years the technology we have available as cameramen has changed massively for the better, but the skills and craft that have to be applied to produce great films has changed very little. It has been wonderful to observe the younger members of our camera teams developing their skills and craft, driven by a desire to continue to give our films the look the audience has grown to love.

AN IDEA TAKES SHAPE

At the heart of every great film is a cracking idea. The details can change, evolve and mutate during production, but if the original vision is right, everything else will fall into place. Unfortunately, ideas are not two-a-penny. They also cannot be summoned to order. Most Aardman artists keep a sketchbook to hand – not just at their desk, but in their rucksack, on the bus or next to their armchair. Wallace & Gromit creator Nick Park says that he is constantly doodling. Sketching like this enables him to have a free flow of thinking, encouraging ideas to emerge naturally without the need to probe and dissect every passing notion. These sketchbooks and early concept pieces are crucial to the filmmaking process. This is where the art of Aardman begins…

In these sketchbook pages, characters have the space to 'evolve', while storylines and atmospheres can be playfully imagined. Here we can see Wallace experimentally wearing a moustache, or Gromit when he still had teeth. From *Chicken Run*, we see a poster of Rocky as he might have appeared in his career as a 'chicken cannonball'. In fact in early versions of the script, we saw quite a lot of his life before he escaped from the circus.

Both pages:
Peter Lord
Morph sketchbook
*The Amazing Adventures
of Morph*, 1980

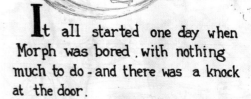

It all started one day when Morph was bored, with nothing much to do - and there was a knock at the door.

"Come in," drawled Morph, lowering his glass. The door opened and Folly entered. Her foil was crumpled, she'd been crying.

"Oh Morph," she gasped, falling forward into his arms. Grimly he clutched her frail shoulders, anger rising within him. "Dusty...he...he."
in

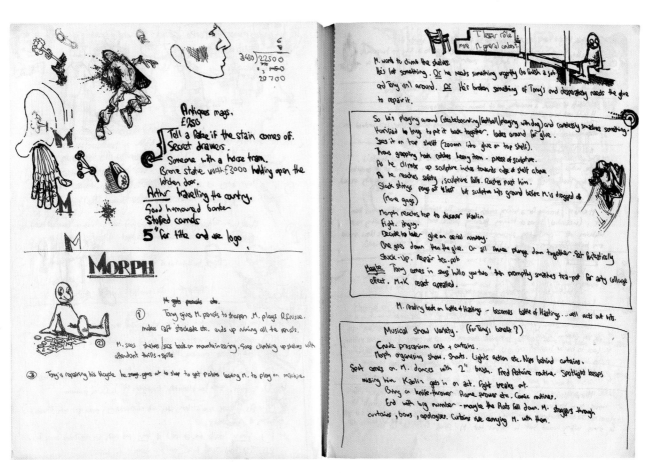

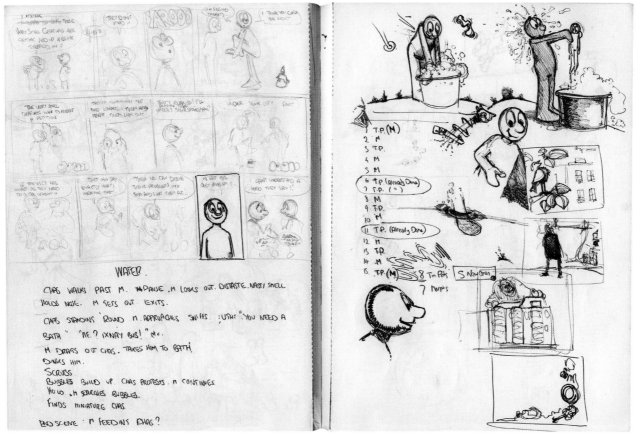

Both pages:
Peter Lord
Morph sketchbook
The Amazing Adventures of Morph, 1980

EXT. BANANA LANDSCAPE. 'A GRAND DAY OUT'.

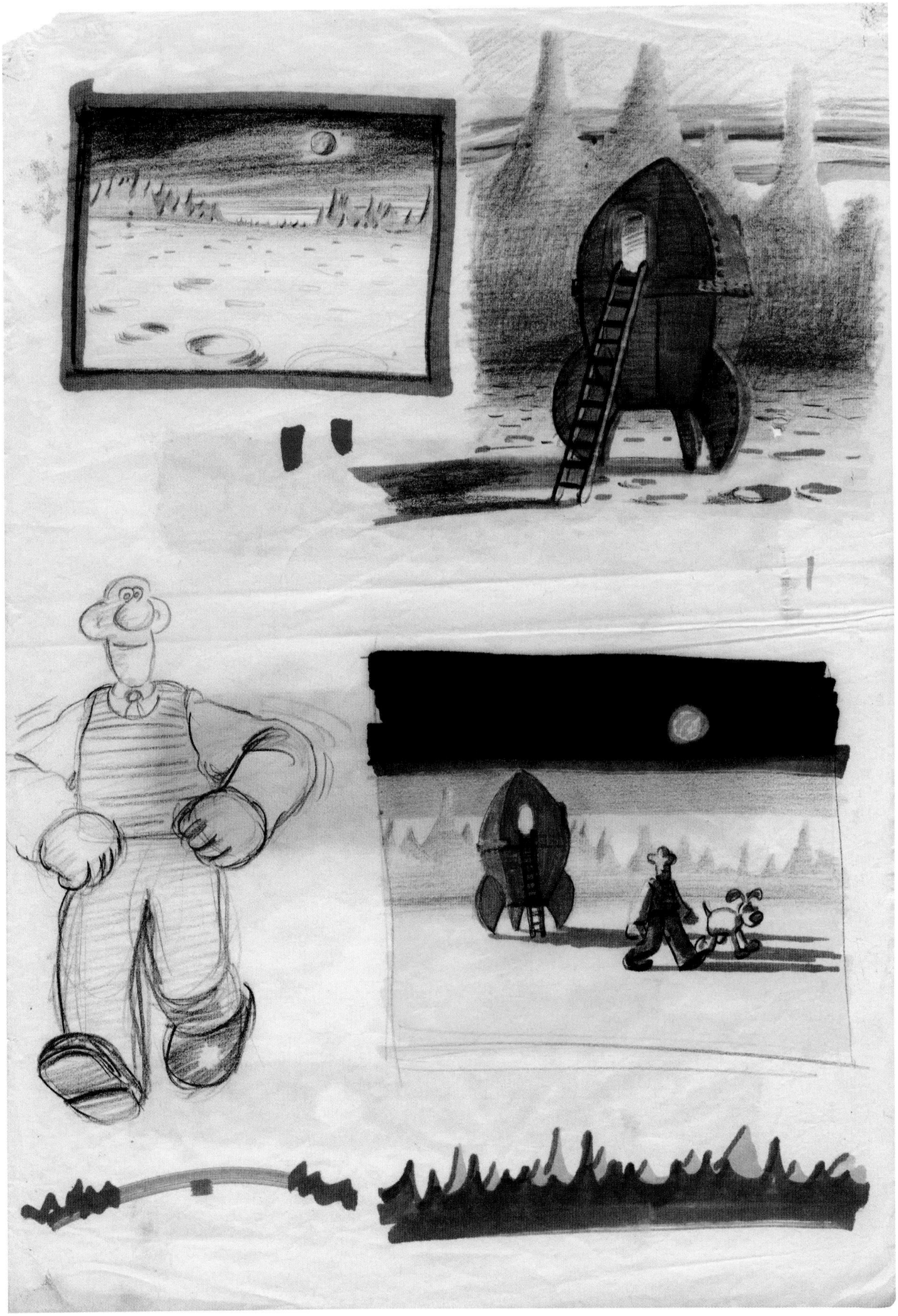

Both pages:
Nick Park
Character study
A Grand Day Out, 1989

Christian Schellewald
Rita's boat, study
Flushed Away, 2006

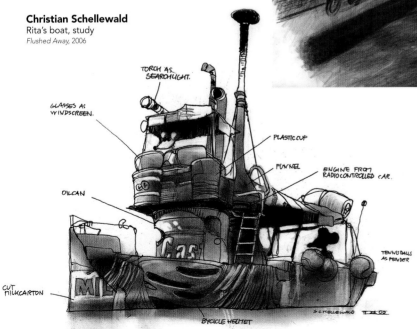

TORCH AS
SEARCHLIGHT.

GLASSES AS
WINDSCREEN.

PLASTIC CUP

FUNNEL

OILCAN

ENGINE FROM
RADIO CONTROLLED CAR.

TENNIS BALLS
AS FENDER

CUT
MILKCARTON

BYCICLE HELMET

SCHELLEWALD

...SHED AWAY. INSPIRATIONAL SKETCH. RITA'S BOAT.

This page, top:
Brizzi
Concept art
Flushed Away, 2006

This page, centre:
Brizzi
Concept art
Flushed Away, 2006

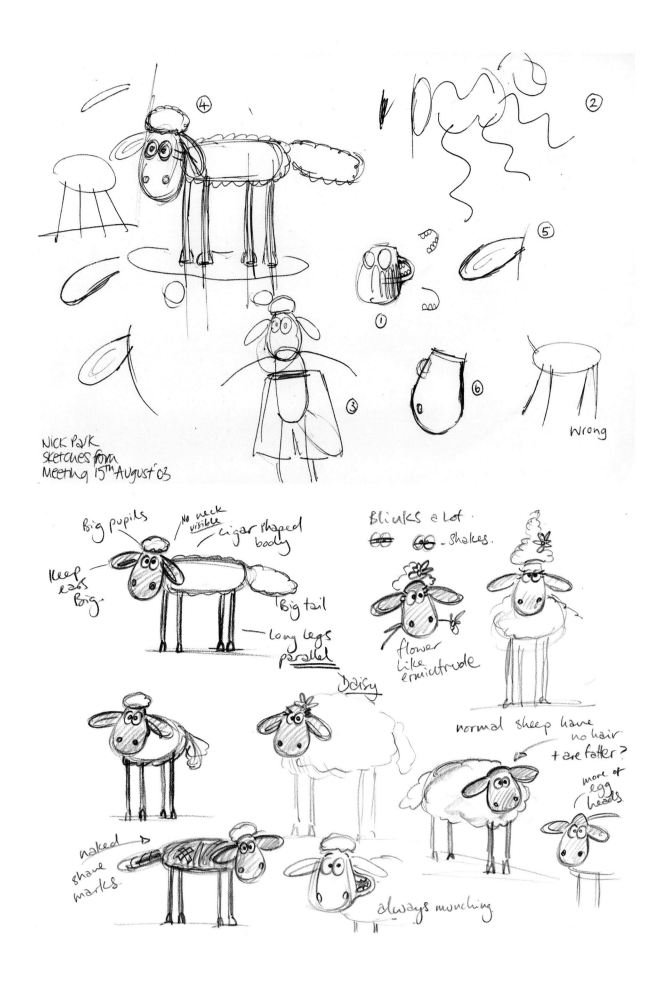

NICK Park
Sketches from
Meeting 15TH August '03

Wrong

Big pupils
No neck visible
cigar shaped body
Keep ears Big
Big tail
Long legs parallel

Blinks a lot.
- shakes.
flower like ermintrude

Daisy

normal sheep have no hair.
+ are fatter?
more of egg heads.

naked shave marks

always munching

22

This page, top:
Michael Salter
Character study
Creature Comforts, series 1, 2003

This page, bottom:
Nick Park
Character study
Heat Electric advertisement, 1991

.mischievous octopii

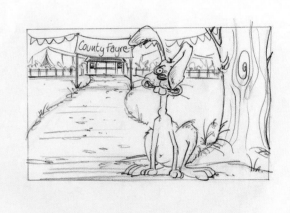

This page, top left:
Sylvia Bennion
Character study
Creature Comforts, series 1, 2003

This page, top right:
Sylvia Bennion
Character study
Creature Comforts, series 1, 2003

This page, centre left:
Michael Salter
Character study
Creature Comforts, series 1, 2003

This page, centre right:
Sylvia Bennion
Character study
Creature Comforts, series 1, 2003

This page, bottom:
Michael Salter
Character study
Creature Comforts, series 1, 2003

Monkeys III

A drawing

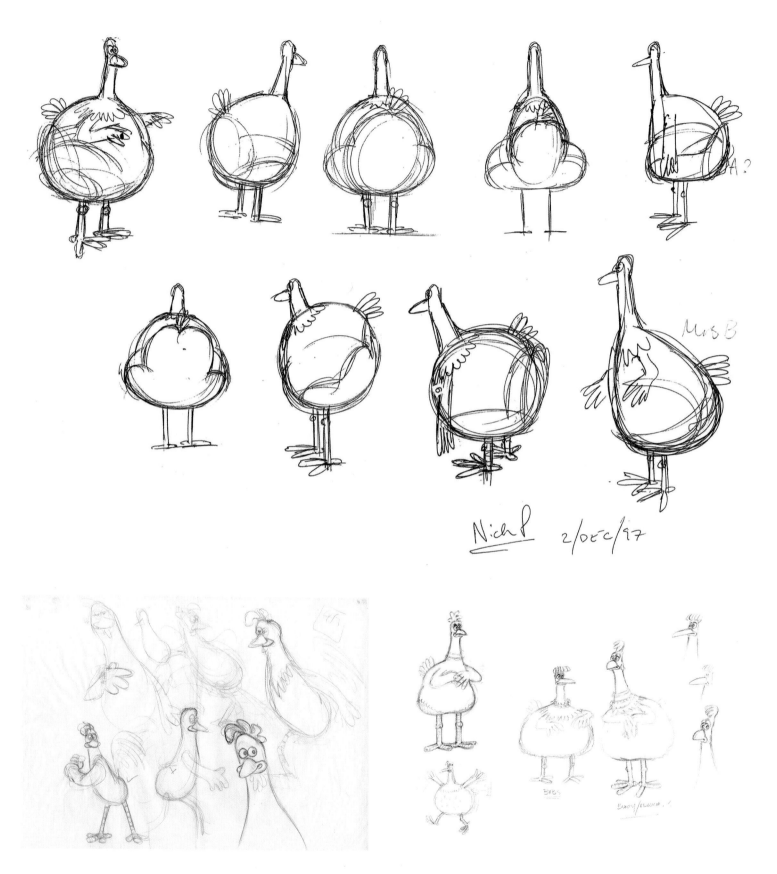

Nick P 2/DEC/97

Facing page, top:
Nick Park
Chickens, character study
Chicken Run, 2000

Facing page, bottom left:
Peter Lord
Rocky, character study
Chicken Run, 2000

Facing page, bottom right:
Nick Park
Bunty and Babs, character
studies
Chicken Run, 2000

This page, top left:
Michael Salter
Character study
Chicken Run, 2000

This page, top right:
David Soren
Rocky's circus costume
Chicken Run, 2000

This page, bottom:
Michael Salter
Rocky and Ginger,
character studies
Chicken Run, 2000

ROCKY'S CIRCUS COSTUME

This page, top left:
Michael Salter
Character study
The Curse of the Were-Rabbit, 2005

This page, top right:
David Vinicombe
Character study
The Curse of the Were-Rabbit, 2005

This page, bottom:
Simon Holland
Study for the graveyard set
The Curse of the Were-Rabbit, 2005

Facing page:
Steve Box
Character study
The Curse of the Were-Rabbit, 2005

TRISTRAM TOTTINGTON

A MARROW OF LIFE AND DEATH

CHAPTER TWO
GETTING INTO CHARACTER

All of Aardman's film stars begin their life on paper. Drawings and character studies allow artists to play with proportion, expression and attitude. This developing visual identity also inspires the writing process. As a character takes shape, narration and form become mixed. Shaun the Sheep's blank peeping eyes, Lady Tottington's delicate, toothy smile and Grand Santa's bony gait are integral to their stories. Character development does not stop here, however. The evolution continues during the transition from 2D art to 3D modelling clay, until a point is reached where the fully rounded personality is ready to make their debut on-screen.

At the earliest stage, nothing is fixed or decided. Look at the versions of Lady Tottington's hair – and indeed her nose. In an early pencil sketch she's even imagined as a Pre-Raphaelite beauty. In the case of *The Pirates!*, the original book by Gideon Defoe referred constantly to the Pirate Captain's 'luxuriant beard', so his character design always places great emphasis on enormous, curly facial hair.

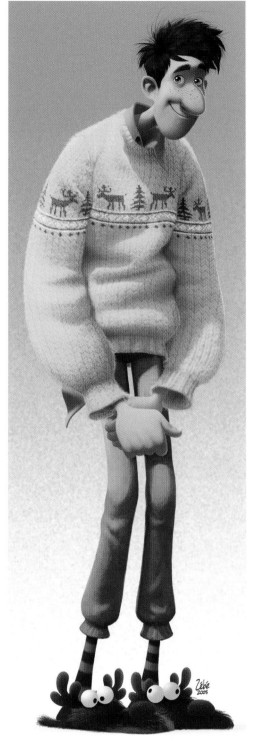

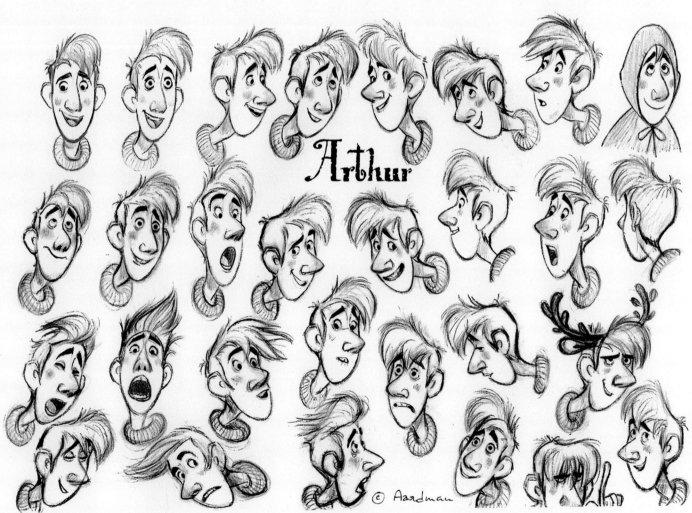

Facing page, left:
Peter de Sève
Arthur, character study
Arthur Christmas, 2011

Facing page, centre:
Peter de Sève
Arthur, character study
Arthur Christmas, 2011

Facing page, right:
Zébé
Arthur, character study
Arthur Christmas, 2011

This page, all:
Carlos Grangel
Arthur, character study
Arthur Christmas, 2011

CRANSANTA

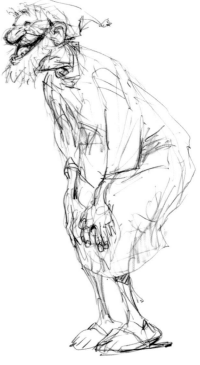

This page:
Peter de Sève
Grand Santa, character study
Arthur Christmas, 2011

Facing page:
Peter de Sève
Dasher, character study
Arthur Christmas, 2011

Facing page:
Peter Lord
Mr Tweedy, character study
Chicken Run, 2000

Facing page:
Peter Lord
Rats, character studies
Chicken Run, 2000

Both pages:
Peter Lord
Rats, character studies
Flushed Away, 2006

Facing page, top left:
Rocky, puppet
Chicken Run, 2000

Facing page, top right:
Michael Salter
Rocky, character study
Chicken Run, 2000

Facing page, bottom left:
Model-maker tools
Chicken Run, 2000

Facing page, bottom right:
Rocky, puppet
Chicken Run, 2000

This page:
Nick Park
Wallace and Gromit,
character studies
A Grand Day Out, 1989

This page:
Richard Starzak
Shaun, character study
Shaun the Sheep TV series, 2007

Facing page, top left:
Sylvia Bennion
Shaun, character study
Shaun the Sheep TV series, 2007

Facing page, top right:
Richard Starzak
Shaun, character study
Shaun the Sheep TV series, 2007

Facing page, centre left:
Richard Starzak
Shaun, character study
Shaun the Sheep TV series, 2007

Facing page, centre right:
Richard Starzak
Cockerel, character study
Shaun the Sheep TV series, 2007

Facing page, bottom left:
Richard Starzak
Shaun, character study
Shaun the Sheep TV series, 2007

Facing page, bottom right:
Nick Park
Shaun, character study
Shaun the Sheep TV series, 2007

EfS + shaunt 15 %.

Shaun cant sleep. guilt.

Shaunski.

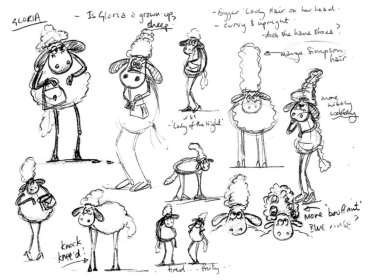

GLORIA

- Is Gloria a grown up sheep?

- Bigger 'Lady Hair on her head.
- curvy & upright
- does she have shoes?

- Marge Simpson hair

'Lady of the Night'

more wibbery wobbery

knock knee'd

tired... fruity

More 'bouffant' BLUE rinse?

HAIR

BUNNY GIRL

44

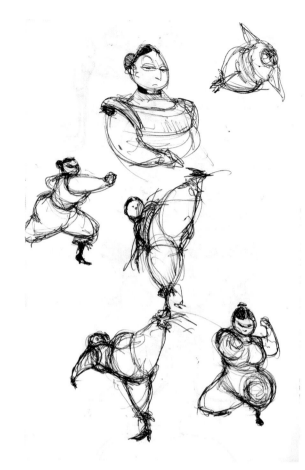

Top left:
Peter Lord
Pirate Captain, character
study
*The Pirates! In an Adventure
with Scientists!,* 2012

Top right:
Peter Lord
Character study
*The Pirates! In an Adventure
with Scientists!,* 2012

Bottom left:
Peter Lord
Character study
*The Pirates! In an Adventure
with Scientists!,* 2012

Bottom right:
Peter Lord
Character study
*The Pirates! In an Adventure
with Scientists!,* 2012

Top:
Jonny Duddle
Charles Darwin, character study
The Pirates! In an Adventure with Scientists!, 2012

Bottom left:
Peter Lord
Charles Darwin, character study
The Pirates! In an Adventure with Scientists!, 2012

Bottom right:
Jonny Duddle
Charles Darwin, character study
The Pirates! In an Adventure with Scientists!, 2012

Top left:
Jonny Duddle
Polly, character study
The Pirates! In an Adventure with Scientists!, 2012

Top right:
Jonny Duddle
Polly, character study
The Pirates! In an Adventure with Scientists!, 2012

Bottom left:
Peter Lord
Victoria, character study
The Pirates! In an Adventure with Scientists!, 2012

Bottom right:
Jonny Duddle
The Surprisingly Curvaceous Pirate, character study
The Pirates! In an Adventure with Scientists!, 2012

CHAPTER THREE
A WHOLE NEW WORLD

Aardman animators don't just tell stories, they whisk us away to strange and amazing places. Even the most mundane setting has a fascinating underside that can enrich our connection with the characters on-screen. Think of Wallace's little red brick terrace that shrouds an enormous rocket building lab in the basement, or the labyrinth of London sewers in *Flushed Away*, occupied by a community just as diverse and thriving as the city above the surface. Over time, drawings and technical plans, atmospheric concept art and skilful model-making combine to create fully immersive worlds for the characters to explore.

Colour, texture and expressive lighting effects all contribute to the creation of a believable new realm. Production designers and art directors look in every direction for research and inspiration – often to classic images from world cinema. In *Chicken Run* for instance, inspiration was taken equally from British landscape paintings of the fifties, visits to the Yorkshire Dales and classic WWII prisoner-of-war tales such as *The Great Escape*.

'Whack-a-Mole'

'Tractor!'

- Shaun is in hot pursuit...

- Timmy manages to upset all the farm animals.

Biter's replacement!
mean looking + nasty 'FANG'

- a sheep worrier.

Biter has stolen pistol

(B.F.S. doesn't run...)

the FARMER

too Barney Rubble...

with glasses

too trainspotter?

All this page:
Sylvia Bennion
Character studies
Shaun the Sheep TV series, 2007

Top left:
Sylvia Bennion
Bitzer, character study
Shaun the Sheep TV series, 2007

Top right:
Richard Starzak
Bitzer, character study
Shaun the Sheep TV series, 2007

Bottom:
Sylvia Bennion
Bitzer, character study
Shaun the Sheep TV series, 2007

Both pages:
Richard Edmunds
Timmy's Nursery
Timmy Time, 2009

Top:
Norman Garwood
Ship interior
The Pirates! In an Adventure with Scientists!, 2012

Centre left:
Peter Lord
Ship interior
The Pirates! In an Adventure with Scientists!, 2012

Bottom left:
Peter Lord
Ship interior
The Pirates! In an Adventure with Scientists!, 2012

Bottom right:
Norman Garwood
Plan for the Pirate Captain's cabin
The Pirates! In an Adventure with Scientists!, 2012

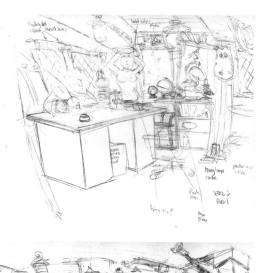

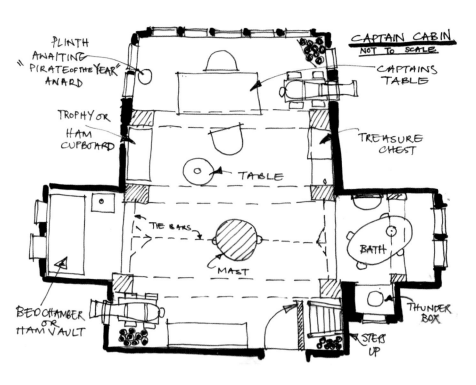

Top left:
Dominique Louis
Captain's cabin
The Pirates! In an Adventure with Scientists!, 2012

Top right:
Adam Cootes
Ship interior
The Pirates! In an Adventure with Scientists!, 2012

Bottom:
The Pirate Captain's cabin
Production still
The Pirates! In an Adventure with Scientists!, 2012

Both pages:
Alfred Llupia
Concept art
*The Pirates! In an Adventure with
Scientists!*, 2012

Top:
Steve Box, Michael Salter
Gromit in the greenhouse
The Curse of the Were-Rabbit, 2005

Bottom left:
Nick Park, Michael Salter
Gromit and the vegetable patch
The Curse of the Were-Rabbit, 2005

Bottom righ:
Nick Park, Michael Salter, Sylvia Bennion
Gromit and the footprint
The Curse of the Were-Rabbit, 2005

Top left:
Nick Park
Study for scene
The Curse of the Were-Rabbit, 2005

Top right:
Michael Salter
Study for scene
The Curse of the Were-Rabbit, 2005

Bottom:
Gromit waters the
vegetables
Production still
The Curse of the Were-Rabbit, 2005

Facing page, top:
Tottington Hall
Production still
The Curse of the Were-Rabbit, 2005

Facing page, bottom left:
Gavin Lines
Family shields, study
The Curse of the Were-Rabbit, 2005

Facing page, bottom right:
Sylvia Bennion
Study for scene
The Curse of the Were-Rabbit, 2005

This page, both:
Sylvia Bennion
Study for scene
The Curse of the Were-Rabbit, 2005

This page, all top:
Michael Salter
Character studies
Chicken Run, 2000

This page, bottom:
Roger Hall
Hen houses, study
Chicken Run, 2000

Facing page, top:
Michael Salter
Hen houses, study
Chicken Run, 2000

Facing page, bottom:
Michael Salter
Rocky and the Pie
Machine, study
Chicken Run, 2000

Facing page, both:
Matt Perry
City, study
Shaun the Sheep Movie, 2015

This page, both:
Alfred Llupia
Concept art
Shaun the Sheep Movie, 2015

Both pages:
Nick Park
Wallace and Gromit,
character studies
A Grand Day Out, 1989

CHAPTER FOUR
AN EYE FOR EVERY DETAIL

It is the artistic richness in every shot that sets Aardman apart from other animation studios. Every environment is meticulously researched, dressed and assembled, giving the films a depth and authenticity. The long list of props, paintings and accessories that appear on-screen is very similar to what viewers might use themselves everyday – each a tiny scale model brought to life by a vast team of talented craftspeople. Each new piece presents an opportunity for the artist to enhance the storytelling or add some of their own quirky humour. Whether it's an ominous WANTED sign for a penguin, a faux Grecian column in an English country house or a minute piece of pirate ship paraphernalia, each has a unique role to play.

Norman Garwood designed the Pirate Ship as if it had been crudely lashed together in a ships' scrapyard from two completely different vessels. The stern was approximately 17th century Dutch, while the foreparts came from a much later frigate. The garden shed on the stern and the gigantic figurehead were clearly also acquired on the cheap. In this instance, the ship itself represented the history of the pirate crew and their many years of unsuccessful plundering. The Were-Rabbit, along with other unlikely monsters designed in the style of primitive woodcuts, all appeared for a fraction of a second in *The Curse of the Were-Rabbit* as the Vicar turned the pages of 'The Observer's Book of Monsters'.

Facing page:
Blood Island stores
Production still
The Pirates! In an Adventure with Scientists!, 2012

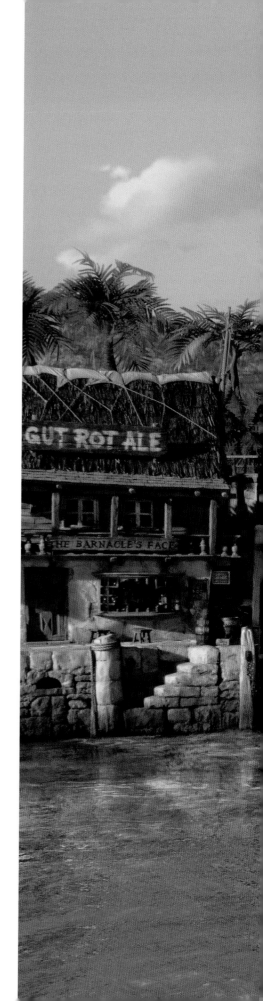

This page, all:
Nick Park
Feathers McGraw,
character study
The Wrong Trousers, 1993

Facing page, top:
Nick Park
Feathers McGraw,
character study
The Wrong Trousers, 1993

Facing page, bottom:
Nick Park
Feathers McGraw and
Gromit, character studies
The Wrong Trousers, 1993

POLICE NOTICE
WANTED

HAVE YOU SEEN
THIS CHICKEN

£1,000 REWARD

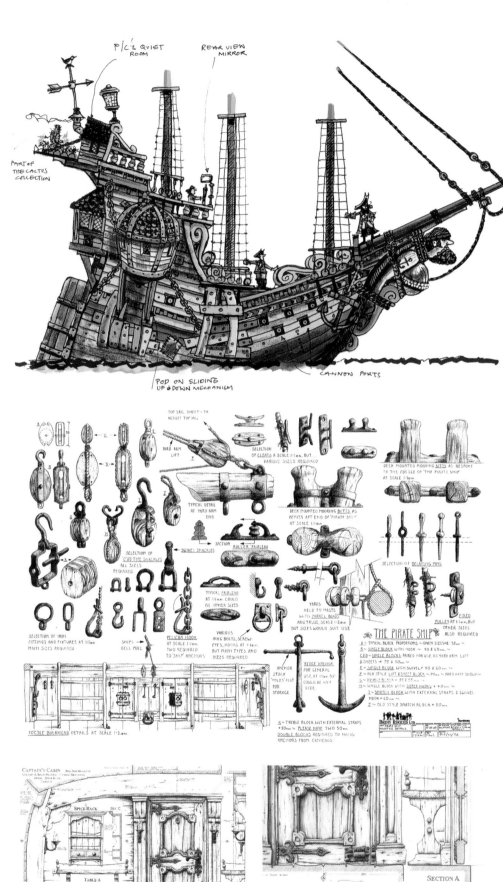

This page, top:
Norman Garwood
Pirate ship, study
The Pirates! In an Adventure with Scientists!, 2012

This page, centre left:
Phil Lewis
Ship details, study
The Pirates! In an Adventure with Scientists!, 2012

This page, centre right:
Matt Sanders
Ship details, study
The Pirates! In an Adventure with Scientists!, 2012

This page, bottom left:
Matt Sanders
Ship details, study
The Pirates! In an Adventure with Scientists!, 2012

This page, bottom centre:
Jonny Duddle
Ship details, study
The Pirates! In an Adventure with Scientists!, 2012

This page, bottom right:
Jonny Duddle
Ship details, study
The Pirates! In an Adventure with Scientists!, 2012

Facing page:
The Pirate Ship
Set model
The Pirates! In an Adventure with Scientists!, 2012

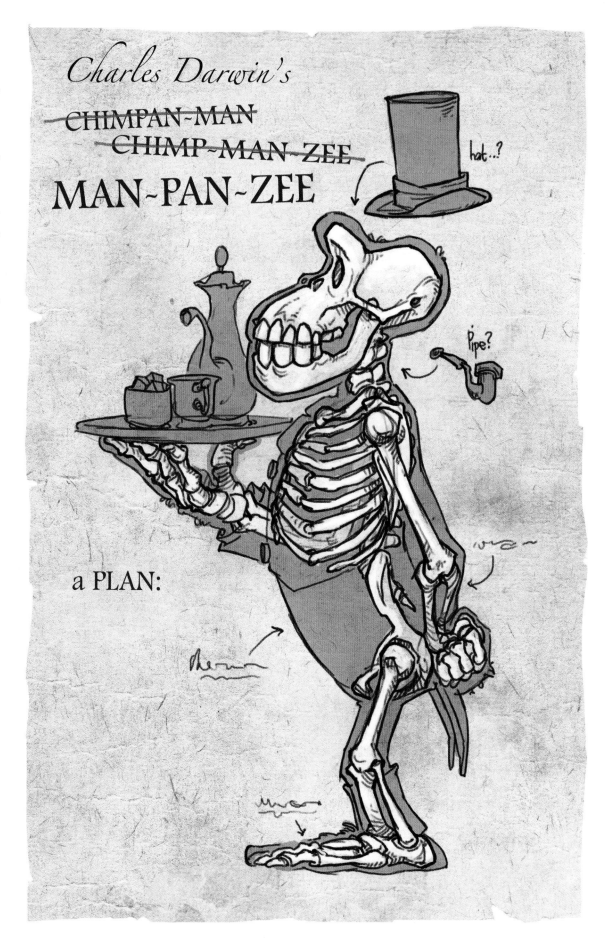

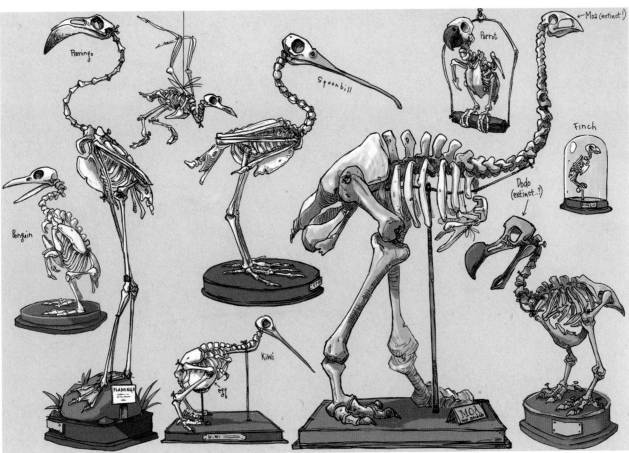

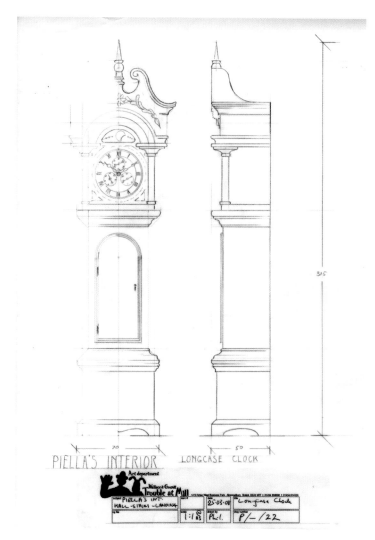

PIELLA'S INTERIOR   LONGCASE CLOCK

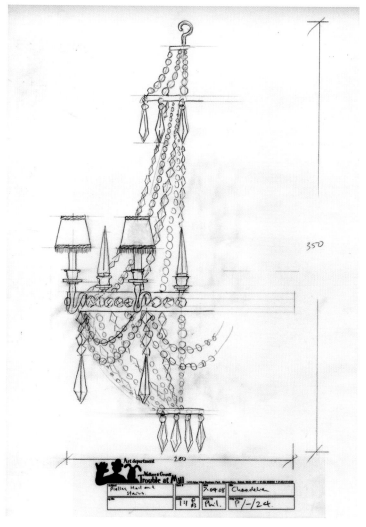

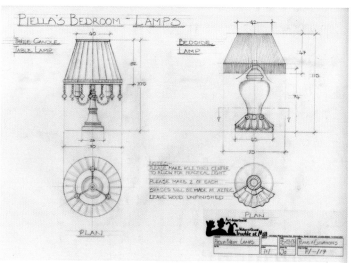

PIELLA'S BEDROOM ~ LAMPS

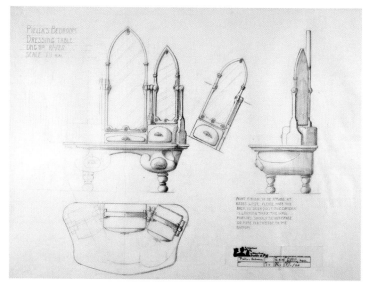

This page, both top:
Phil Lewis
Technical drawing for props
A Matter of Loaf and Death, 2008

This page, bottom left:
Jo Symanowski
Technical drawing for props
A Matter of Loaf and Death, 2008

This page, bottom right:
Phil Lewis
Technical drawing for props
A Matter of Loaf and Death, 2008

Both pages:
Gavin Lines
Designs for 'Book of
Monsters' prop
The Curse of the Were-Rabbit, 2005

Facing page, top left:
Lady Tottington makes a call
Production still
The Curse of the Were-Rabbit, 2005

Facing page, top right:
In the lift
Production still
The Curse of the Were-Rabbit, 2005

Facing page, bottom:
Interior of Tottington Hall
Production still
The Curse of the Were-Rabbit, 2005

This page, top:
Lady Tottington's greenhouse
Production still
The Curse of the Were-Rabbit, 2005

This page, bottom left:
Lady Tottington's greenhouse
Production still
The Curse of the Were-Rabbit, 2005

This page, bottom right:
The Were-rabbit and Lady
Tottington
Production still
The Curse of the Were-Rabbit, 2005

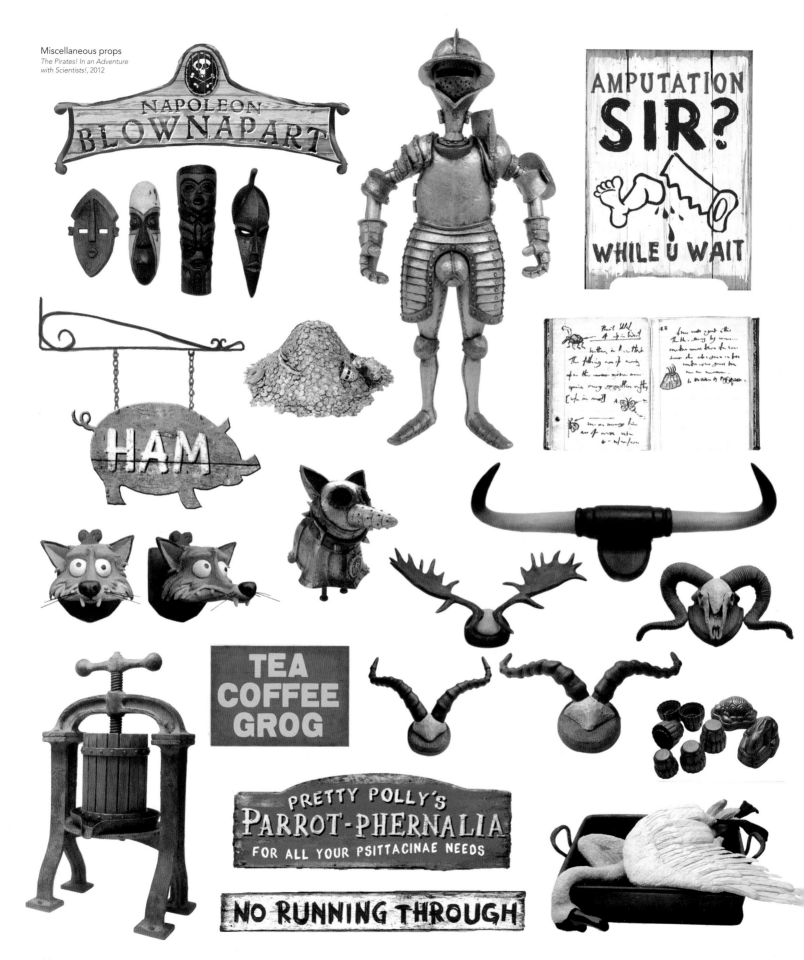

NAPOLEON BLOWNAPART

AMPUTATION SIR? WHILE U WAIT

HAM

TEA COFFEE GROG

PRETTY POLLY'S PARROT-PHERNALIA FOR ALL YOUR PSITTACINAE NEEDS

NO RUNNING THROUGH

Live SPORTS Crab Racing this Thursday

WORLD'S BEST CAPTAIN

'HOP-ALONG' HAWKINS
BESPOKE CRUTCHES • WOODEN LEGS

MODEL VILLAGE
100 YDS

R. SPANKER
FUTTOCKS   ROLLOCKS
MAST RAISERS
& SHIP SUPPLIES
RIGGING   TACKLE

CHAPTER FIVE
MECHANICAL MARVELS

The world of Aardman is crammed full of amazing contraptions. Where else could you see an automated chicken pot pie maker, a pair of remote-controlled trousers or a thought bending Mind Manipulation-O-Matic gizmo in action? The studio uses both technical and artistic methods to create its marvellous, mind-blogging, often malfunctioning machines. Detailed scale drawings, intricate models and Leonardo De Vinci style pencil impressions combine to create devices that whir, click and buzz before our very eyes. The result? Flabbergasting ingenuity, astonishing engineering and bucketloads of humour.

Wallace's wonderful, riveted moon rocket has all the comforts of home including – uniquely in the annals of space exploration – curtains and wallpaper. Some of the same homemade warmth has determined the design of Santa's classic sleigh from *Arthur Christmas*, contrasting starkly with the cold efficiency of the new Super-Sleigh.

Facing page:
The Mind Manipulation-O-
Matic
Production still
The Curse of the Were-Rabbit, 2005

'PORRIDGE GUN'

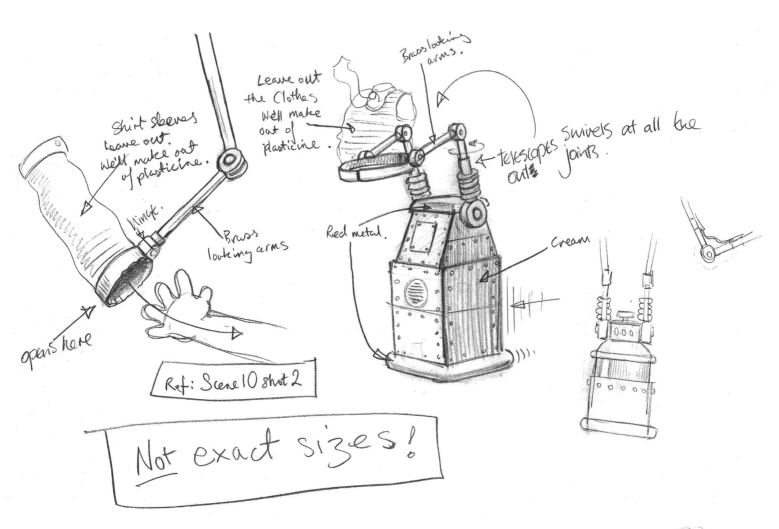

Shirt sleeves leave out. We'll make out of plasticine.

hinge.

opens here

Brass looking arms

Ref: Scene 10 shot 2

Leave out the Clothes We'll make out of Plasticine.

Brass looking arms.

telescopes swivels at all the out joints.

Red metal.

Cream

Not exact sizes!

Facing page, top left:
Michael Salter
Contraptions, study
Cracking Contraptions, 2002

Facing page, top right:
Nick Park
Contraptions, study
Cracking Contraptions, 2002

Facing page, bottom left:
Michael Salter
Contraptions, study
Cracking Contraptions, 2002

Facing page, bottom right:
Nick Park
Contraptions, study
Cracking Contraptions, 2002

This page, top:
Nick Park
Contraptions, study
Cracking Contraptions, 2002

This page, bottom:
Nick Park
Contraptions, study
Cracking Contraptions, 2002

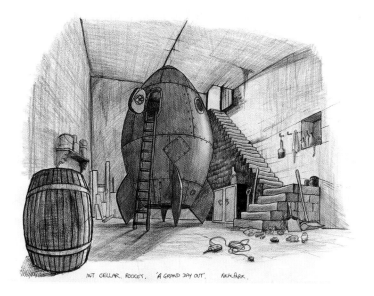

INT. CELLAR. ROCKET. 'A GRAND DAY OUT'. NICK PARK.

Both pages:
Nick Park
Wallace and Gromit,
character studies
A Grand Day Out, 1989

Facing page, bottom left:
Nick Park
Rocket, study
A Grand Day Out, 1989

Facing page, bottom right:
Nick Park
Rocket, study
A Grand Day Out, 1989

This page:
Nick Park
Rocket, study
A Grand Day Out, 1989

This page:
The rocket
Set model
A Grand Day Out, 1989

Facing page:
Nick Park
Rocket, study
A Grand Day Out, 1989

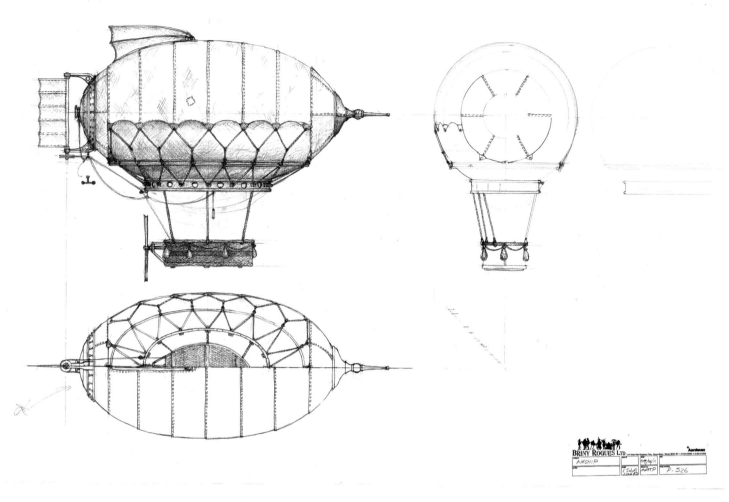

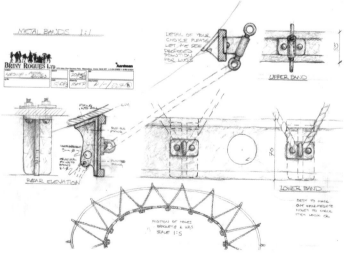

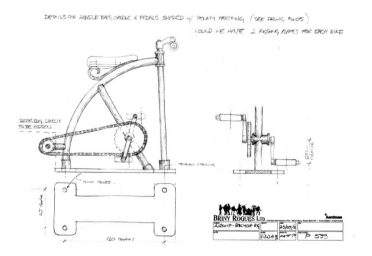

This page, all:

Matt Perry
Darwin's airship,
technical drawings
*The Pirates! In an Adventure
with Scientists!*, 2012

Facing page:
The Pirate Captain spies
land ahoy
Production still
*The Pirates! In an Adventure
with Scientists!*, 2012

Facing page, top left:
Michael Salter
Flying machine, study
Chicken Run, 2000

Facing page, top right:
Peter Lord
Flying machine, study
Chicken Run, 2000

Facing page, bottom:
Nick Park
Flying machine, study
Chicken Run, 2000

This page, top:
Michael Salter
Chickens in flying
machine, study
Chicken Run, 2000

This page, bottom:
Michael Salter
Flying machine, study
Chicken Run, 2000

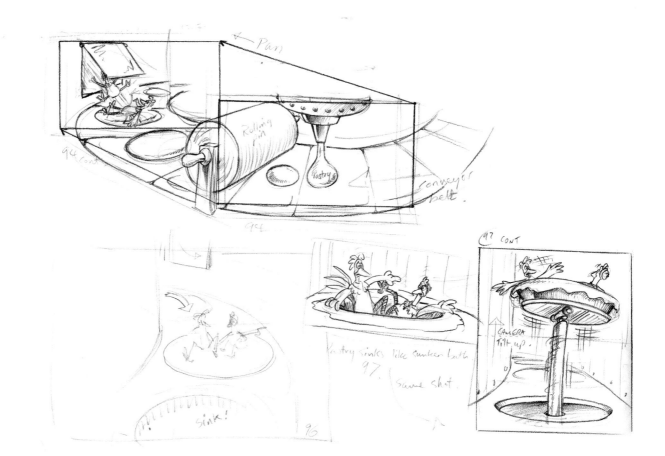

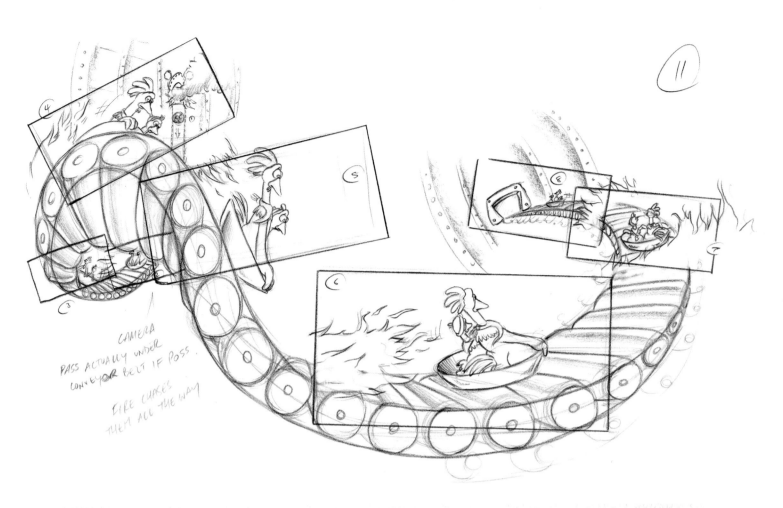

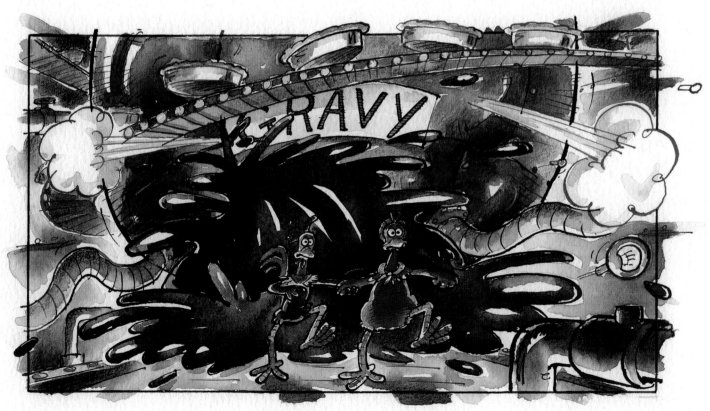

This page, all:
Nick Park
Top Bun, studies
A Matter of Loaf and Death, 2008

Facing page:
Michael Salter
Anti-Pesto car
A Matter of Loaf and Death, 2008

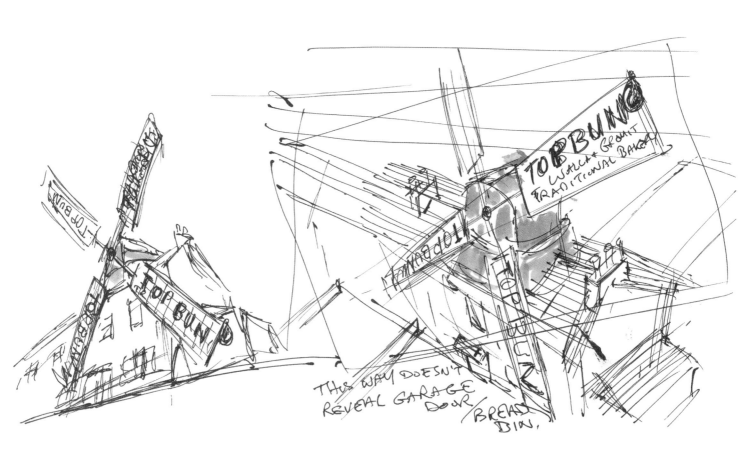

THIS WAY DOESN'T REVEAL GARAGE DOOR / BREAD BIN.

This page, top:
James Lee, Evgeni Tomov
Concept art
Arthur Christmas, 2011

This page, bottom:
Evgeni Tomov
Concept art
Arthur Christmas, 2011

Facing page, both:
Evgeni Tomov
Concept art
Arthur Christmas, 2011

CHAPTER SIX

A LOVE AFFAIR WITH LIGHT

Facing page:
Gromit arrives at Piella's mansion
Production still
A Matter of Loaf and Death, 2008

Lighting is both a technique and an art – the critical element that brings a film to life. It has been a source of constant intrigue to David Sproxton, and something that Peter Lord simply calls 'a joy'. Working with scale models that are often just a fifth of life-size makes lighting a shot even more of a sublime challenge. When it works however, the results can create a piece of cinema that stirs both hearts and minds. Light on sculpture can highlight a curve, throw a character silhouette into sharp relief or cast a shadow full of portent and meaning. It is a fine art that enables the animator to breathe life into his or her puppet, silently expressing what they might be thinking or feeling. It is painstaking, essential work – the final touch that makes the illusion real as it flickers before us on-screen.

Both pages:
Dominique Louis
Concept art
The Pirates! In an Adventure with Scientists!, 2012

Facing page:
Queen Victoria looks up
Production still
The Pirates! In an Adventure with Scientists!, 2012

This page, top:
The throne room
Production still
The Pirates! In an Adventure with Scientists!, 2012

This page, centre:
Polly and the pirates
Production still
The Pirates! In an Adventure with Scientists!, 2012

This page, bottom:
Tavern talk
Production still
The Pirates! In an Adventure with Scientists!, 2012

This page, top:
Stephen Hanson
Concept art
Arthur Christmas, 2011

This page, centre:
**Stephen Hanson,
Evgeni Tomov**
Concept art
Arthur Christmas, 2011

This page, bottom:
**Desmond Downes,
Evgeni Tomov**
Concept art
Arthur Christmas, 2011

Facing page, top:
Evgeni Tomov
Concept art
Arthur Christmas, 2011

Facing page, bottom:
**Stephen Hanson,
Evgeni Tomov**
Concept art
Arthur Christmas, 2011

Main image:
**Mr and Mrs Tweedy count
their chickens**
Production still
Chicken Run, 2000

This page, top:
Solitary confinement
Production still
Chicken Run, 2000

Michael Salter
Wallace, character study
The Curse of the Were-Rabbit,
2005

Michael Salter.

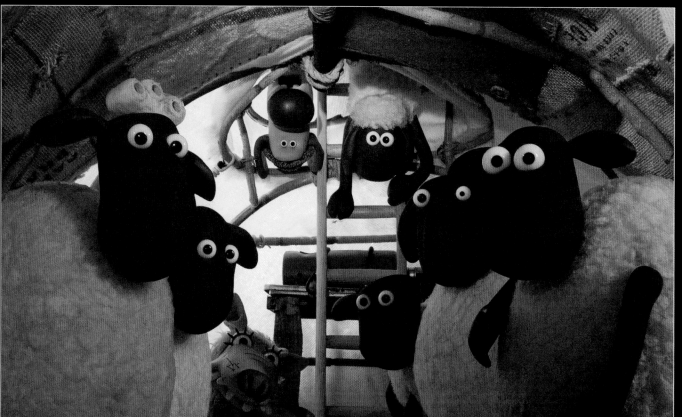

Facing page, top:
The Farmer rides out of the city
Production still
Shaun the Sheep Movie, 2015

Facing page, bottom:
Inside the pantomime horse
Production still
Shaun the Sheep Movie, 2015

This page, top:
Moonlight chase
Production still
Shaun the Sheep Movie, 2015

This page, bottom:
The Farmer and his flock
Production still
Shaun the Sheep Movie, 2015

Next page:
Sheep in the big city
Set shot
Shaun the Sheep Movie, 2015

ACKNOWLEDGEMENTS

This amazing book could not have been created without the help of a dedicated and diligent team. Thank you to Peter Lord and David Sproxton for your inspiring forewords and support. We are very grateful to Tom Vincent and Mollie Bowen, the Aardman archivists, and of course to the many wonderful artists who have worked on the films over the years. We'd like to acknowledge the hard work of the Rights team – Rob Goodchild, Sean Clarke, Laura Daniel, Laura Burr, Jess Houston, Danny Heffer and Hannah MacFarlane. Thanks to Iain MacGregor at Simon & Schuster UK and Stephanie Bramwell-Lawes at Imago. And last, but definitely not least, to writer and editor Mandy Archer and Nick Avery Design for putting such a beautiful book together for us!

PICTURE CREDITS